EXTREME WEATHER SYSTEMS
3RD GRADE GEOGRAPHY SERIES

Extreme weather includes unusual, severe or unseasonal weather.

A thunderstorm is a type of storm characterized by the presence of lightning and its acoustic effect on the Earth's atmosphere known as thunder.

Tornadoes are sometimes called twisters. A tornado is a rapidly spinning tube of air that touches both the ground and a cloud above.

A waterspout
is an intense
columnar vortex
that occurs over
a body of water.
Waterspouts exist
on a microscale,
where their
environment is
less than two
kilometers in
width.

Hurricanes are one of the most dangerous natural hazards to people. Hurricanes usually form in tropical areas of the world.

A blizzard is a severe snowstorm that usually has very cold temperatures and high winds.

An ice storm
is a type of
winter storm
characterized
by freezing rain.
The freezing rain
from an ice storm
covers everything
with heavy,
smooth glaze ice.

A heat wave is a prolonged period of excessively hot weather. Extreme heat can cause cramps, swelling, and fainting.